Hairy Lemon
Cookbook

SIMON COOPER

AuthorHouse™ UK
1663 Liberty Drive
Bloomington, IN 47403   USA
www.authorhouse.co.uk
Phone: 0800.197.4150

Interior Photography by Jennifer Oppermann
jenniferoppermann@gmail.com
Front Cover by Thomas Rudys

Illustration by Susan Shorter

Published by AuthorHouse 12/08/2016

ISBN: 978-1-5246-2972-4 (sc)
ISBN: 978-1-5246-2973-1 (e)

Print information available on the last page.

This book is printed on acid-free paper.

authorHOUSE®

Darren Cooper

AUTHOR'S NOTE

The hairy lemon cookbook has come together through decades of preparing delicious and well loved food for the people of Dublin as well as its visitors to the point of The Hairy Lemon Restaurant receiving awards from the city council and being consecutively rated as the best of its kind for traditional food in Dublin. The pub itself is named after a well known street character from the forties who had turned jaundice from drinking too much "poitín", a homemade potato vodka renowned for its potency, and with his beard and the shape of his head, he was said to resemble a hairy lemon.

The menu was originally inspired by my Grand Mother Kathleen who was famous throughout our family for being a fantastic traditional cook. All the kids would eagerly anticipate the regular Sunday visit to Grand Mothers house for her famous roast beef, stews, bread & butter pudding & apples pies. Not typical foods for kids to fight over but hers were that good that to eat her cooking was a real treat. Over the years the Hairy Lemon has broadened its menu to include some different dishes such as our curries and stir fry's but with a mind to keep our Grand Mothers style of cooking alive and well. This however is not all you get with a visit to the Hairy Lemon as our customers know. Our customers are greeted cordially and treated as family and relationships are regularly formed with people from every corner of the globe keeping in regular contact or returning with family to introduce to us from far and away.

We like to have fun and our customers know us for a bit of real Dublin banter in cosy surroundings that make them feel like they're visiting their Grand Mothers with our home made comfort foods that are just always the favourite compared to anything else.

I hope you find this book to be a treasured resource for great food, Irish character and fun.

2016
CERTIFICATE *of*
EXCELLENCE

tripadvisor®

 The Hairy Lemon
5 October at 17:00 · 🌐

We're super delighted to be mentioned by Publin as having one of the best traditional Irish Stew's in Dublin! Thanks very much for the mention guys! http://publin.ie/2016/10-pubs-to-get-the-best-traditional-irish-stew-in-dublin/

10 pubs to get the best traditional Irish stew in Dublin | Publin

Contents

Hairy Lemon

In the first half of the 20th century, Dublin's city centre had a number of "street characters" who were noticed and remarked upon for their individuality and perhaps more so their oddness. This was a time when most people had less money, no television and had recently come into a modern state of living. People had to entertain themselves, with a parlour in the front of the house for visitors where singing and playing of musical instruments was practiced for when in company. There was also the Irish wit which in part consisted of gentle jibes which were only meant in good fun. Our Irish elders often fondly look back and refer to this period as "Dublin City in the rare auld times". There were however a number of stragglers who didn't move with the times as quickly as the rest.

The "Hairy Lemon" was one of the best known of these. He worked for the council catching stray dogs as in those days all wandering unlicensed dogs were rounded up and Hairy Lemon was one of those who did the catching. He had no fixed address and wore a loose cloth cap and a large scarf around his short neck. In the colder months he wore a raincoat fastened with a straw rope and in the summer months an old tweed jacket. He was frequently on the streets due to his profession so he was well known to see by many. He suffered with jaundice, most likely from the love of the drink and when someone remarked that with his yellowish complexion and the shape of his head and his facial hair that he looked like a hairy lemon, the name seemed to just stick and history was made. Children of the time would shout from a safe distance, "Hairy Lemon, has your mother got any more like you?" There have been television shows such as "Strumpet City", songs such as "The Mero" by The Dubliners and works of art which are largely based on individuals like the Hairy Lemon not forgetting that one of today's best pub and restaurants in Dublin is named after the Hairy Lemon.

Another of Dublin's well known street characters was called "Forty coats" who was a kind of hobo who wore everything he owned. The children of the time had a kind of game for a bit of excitement and would run past him and shout, "Hey Forty Coats, how many coats are you wearing today". The aim of the game being to get away without being caught and dealt a swift chastisement.

Yet another of these characters was Known as "Bang Bang". Bang Bang was traumatized from World War One and was known to wander the streets carrying a large old key which he would point and shoot at people. With this particular activity, he was well liked by children and adults alike for causing fun. Children would point their fingers and shoot back at him and it is said that when Bang Bang would travel by bus or tram that within minutes, inevitably, the whole carriage would be having a shootout with each other with their hands.

These characters are a part of Dublin culture which has formed part of our modern Dublin Irish-ness which you have to come to Dublin to really experience for yourself and there is no better place for great traditional Irish food and drink and "the craic" than the Hairy Lemon pub and restaurant. We look forward to your visit.

My mother started the business in the hairy lemon 20 years ago on the 14 Feb and over the years we've been constantly been asked for recipes.

The Irish Shamrock

The Irish shamrock symbol is closely associated with St Patrick, the patron saint of Ireland. St Patrick is believed to have actually been from Scotland or Wales. Irish raiders captured and enslaved him at the end of fourth century. He spent six years in slavery, probably in the west of Ireland. While in captivity, he turned to his religion for comfort and strength. He finally managed to escape and return home. Years later, ordained as a priest, he returned to convert what was at that time pagan Ireland.

The story of the Irish trefoil relates to St Patrick trying to teach the Irish about the Blessed Trinity, the Christian concept of three Gods – Father, Son, and Holy Ghost (Spirit) – in one. As he was struggling to get his message across one day, he picked up a shamrock, a plant believed to be sacred to the Druids, and asked, "Is it one leaf or three?"

"It is both one leaf and three," the people replied. That's how he managed to grab their attention.

People celebrate St Patrick's Day on 17 March each year, commemorating the day St Patrick (supposedly) died. In Ireland, it is a public holiday, and most businesses close. There are colourful parades in most towns throughout the country. This tradition is copied in cities all over the world, wherever there is a sizeable Irish population.

Traditionally, men and women wear a bunch of shamrocks on their lapel on St Patrick's Day. That is less common nowadays among younger people, probably because the shamrock shrivels after a few hours.

"It's not that the Irish are cynical. It's rather that they have a wonderful lack of respect for everything and everybody." Brendan Behan was spot on when he said this, don't you think? The quotes shared at the end of this book are proof of the wonderful things that the Irish can come up with using just the English language.

Dedication

This book is dedicated to my grandparents Michael & Kathleen Bacon & their nine children. My grandfather was a builder & a pillar of his community. He built many things such as schools, local community buildings & Catholic shrines. He grew his own vegetables like cabbage & potatoes which were staples in Irish cuisine & also rhubarb, apples & berries for tarts & cakes, in my grandparents large garden & ensured that the children never wanted for anything. My grandfather was always happy to see his children & even then grandchildren after a hard days' work. My grandmother was the best traditional Irish food cook I've ever known. She knew all the tricks for making a tantalising meal with whatever was available & many of the recipes in this book & in the Hairy Lemon Restaurant are based on these. There was always the smell of delicious stews & cakes being prepared in the house & this food was so good that my cousins & I as children would lick our lips looking forward to our serving unlike a lot of today's kids who rarely stray from eating plain dishes & a fast food diet. Hopefully with the help of this book, we can turn that around. My aunts & uncles often told us about the fun they had toasting fresh home made bread over the flames of the fire as a young family while telling ghost stories & having great family fun. This was like the fun things done on modern camping trips which were done indoors in Ireland due to the lifestyle of the Irish family of the fifties & sixties & also usually the cold Irish climate. The boys learned to play guitar, piano, tin whistle & other instruments such as the mandolin while the girls would learn singing & Irish dancing. Many parties were held with neighbours & friends when all would join in & perform their particular talent for fun & entertainment. The carpet was always taken up for these occasions! So everyone could have a dance. The kids playground was on the street and the park where all the neighbourhood kids would gather & play games like hop scotch, handball, chasing,skipping,football and of course Gaelic football. Usually one of the elder kids on the street would climb a tall lamp post with a rope to make a swing for everyone to use. The garden was made into a stage with whatever props they could find where the kids would perform their version of a film they had gone to see for those who hadn't seen it. The front garden was also used for a "sale of work" for the kids to earn money for treats & outings by gathering bric-a-brack &

presenting it for sale to passers by. Times were much safer then & kids were left to play together & look after themselves until meal times when they would hurry home promptly for their meals. Keys were commonly left in doors & there was a strong sense of community among all. Kids would often find stray animals & the garden would become a bit of a zoo. These were wholesome times. I think we should take from this the value of family & community in which everyone takes part. We should make the most of what's available to us, especially our parents as they're the only ones we have. In today's busy world it's easy to lose track of important things & people but we should make time to try to enjoy life together as our families before us have done because it's not long until time is passed & you'll wish you could turn back the clock.

Illustration by Angela Cooper

Acknowledgements

I would like to thank my mother for the inspiration, motivation & her help in putting this book together & also for her never give up attitude which was the only assistance available to her as a young mother but is what took her from being a single mother with three young children to being a successful entrepreneur who helped to make The Hairy Lemon Pub into the landmark of pilgrimage to Dublin visitors that it is today with consecutive awards for food & service, in book recommendations from the worlds' number one travel guru Rick Steves & regular tweets from the hugely followed Tweeting Goddess, Ted Rubin as well as various accreditations from many sources around the world. I would like to thank Peter Hanahoe, the proprietor of The Hairy Lemon pub for the last twenty years as my mothers' business partner & all the staff of The Hairy Lemon past & present who have helped to make it what it is today. I would like to thank my brother Darren, my sister Melissa & my aunt Annette Cooke for their drive & dedication in making The Hairy Lemon Restaurant the pinnacle it is today as a great place for food, fun & good times for the public.

BREADS

Irish Soda Bread

Ingredients

- 450 grams plain flour
- 1 heaped teaspoon sugar
- 1 heaped teaspoon salt
- 1 teaspoon bicarbonate of soda
- 230 millilitres buttermilk

Method

1. Preheat oven to 230 degrees C.
2. In a large mixing bowl, sift together your dry ingredients.
3. Add your buttermilk gradually and knead together well using your hands or a standing mixer until a dough is formed.
4. Place the dough evenly along the base of a well greased and floured bread baking tin. With a sharp knife, cut an X along the top from corner to corner.
5. Bake in the oven for 15 minutes. Reduce the temperature to 180 degrees C and continue to bake for approximately 25 minutes more. Be careful not to burn.
6. Remove when the bread is well risen and a golden brown crust has formed on top.

Irish Brown Bread

Ingredients

- 500 grams whole wheat flour
- 250 grams white flour
- 1 1/2 teaspoons salt
- 1 1/2 teaspoons baking soda
- 450 millilitres buttermilk or sour milk
- 20 grams butter

Method

1. Preheat oven to 230 degrees C.
2. In a large mixing bowl, thoroughly sift together your dry ingredients.
3. Add your buttermilk and butter gradually and knead together well using your hands or a standing mixer until a dough is formed.
4. Place the dough evenly along the base of a well greased and floured bread baking tin. With a sharp knife, cut an X along the top from corner to corner.
5. Bake in the oven for 20 minutes. Reduce the temperature to 180 degrees C and continue to bake for approximately 20 minutes more. Be careful not to burn.

Irish Potato Bread

This great Irish side, also called fadge, is formed a little like French pastry to create another filler the likes of which would knock out a bull!

Ingredients

- 1 kilogram potatoes, peeled
- 50 millilitres whole milk
- 25 grams butter, plus more for frying
- 1 egg, beaten
- salt and pepper
- 50 grams plain flour
- 1/2 onion, finely diced
- fresh chopped thyme

Method

1. Cook the potatoes in boiling water.
2. When the potatoes are cooked, strain and place back onto a low heat to aid in the removal of moisture. Mash for about 4 minutes.
3. Add your milk, butter, egg, and a good pinch of salt and pepper. Continue to mix until well incorporated.
4. With a lot of elbow grease, gradually mix in the flour until a good dough is formed.
5. Form the dough into a large 1-inch-thick disk and cut into slices.
6. Heat more butter and fry the onion and thyme on a medium heat for 2 minutes. Add your dough slices. Remove when golden and enjoy.

FULL IRISH BREAKFAST

STARTERS

Potato and Leek Soup

This is a most famous Irish soup, with a unique warmth and flavour that can only be described as gorgeous.

Ingredients

- 20 grams butter
- 5 tablespoons chopped fresh parsley
- 450 grams leeks, rinsed and chopped
- 1 onion, chopped
- 1 celery stalk, chopped
- 1 kilograms potatoes, peeled and chopped
- 1 litres chicken stock (2 cubes)
- 500 millilitres whole milk, divided1 bay leaf
- salt and pepper

Method

1. Melt the butter in a large saucepan over a medium heat.
2. Add the parsley, leeks, onion, and celery. Cover and cook for about 5 minutes, stirring frequently, until the onions are soft and golden.
3. Add the potatoes, stock, half the milk, the bay leaf, and a good pinch of salt and pepper.
4. Reduce heat to low, cover, and simmer for about 40 minutes. Make sure your potatoes are well cooked and soft. Remove from the heat.
5. Remove the bay leaf, add the remaining milk, and blend until smooth with a stick blender. Serve and enjoy!

Seafood Chowder

Ingredients

- butter, for frying
- 1 small onion, diced
- 1 leek, trimmed and diced
- 1 small carrot, diced
- 1 potato, cubed
- 120 millilitres white wine
- 450 millilitres fish stock
- 225 grams mixed fresh fish fillets (cod, haddock, hake, or salmon), skinned and cut into bite-sized pieces
- 175 grams raw Dublin bay prawns and mussels, scrubbed clean
- 1 tablespoon chopped fresh flat-leaf parsley
- 175 millilitres cream
- salt and freshly ground black pepper

Method

1. Add some butter to a large saucepan over medium heat. After 1 minute, add the onion, leek, carrot, and potato, Cook for 2 to 3 minutes or until softened slightly.
2. Add the wine and reduce by half.
3. Add the stock. Bring to a simmer, and then add the fish fillets and shellfish.
4. Return to a simmer, and then add the parsley and cream.
5. Cover and cook for 5 minutes. Remove any unopened mussels.
6. Add salt and pepper to taste. Serve hot with buttered brown bread.

Farmhouse Vegetable Soup

A world-famous classic which stands the test of time.

Ingredients

- butter, for frying
- 3 large carrots, peeled and chopped
- 1 large onion, chopped
- 1 leek, rinsed and chopped
- 1 celery stick, rinsed and chopped
- 1 parsnip, peeled and chopped
- 4 large potatoes, peeled and chopped
- 1 litres vegetable stock
- salt and pepper

Method

1. Add some butter to a large pan over low heat. After 1 minute, add your carrots, onion, leek, celery, and parsnip. Cover and cook for about 5 minutes, stirring frequently.
2. Add in your potatoes and your stock. Bring to the boil and then reduce to a low heat.
3. Cover and cook for about 40 minutes or until your potatoes are soft through.
4. Blend until smooth.
5. Add salt and pepper to taste and serve.

Carrot Soup

A light and delicious soup created with a great combination of flavoursome root vegetables.

Ingredients

- butter, for frying
- 800 grams carrots, peeled and sliced
- 2 onions, chopped
- 4 crushed garlic cloves
- 4 tablespoons fresh parsley
- 1 litre vegetable stock
- salt and pepper
- cream and fresh coriander, for garnish

Method

1. Add some butter to a large saucepan over low heat. After 1 minute, add your carrots, onions, garlic, and parsley. Cover and cook, stirring frequently, for 5 minutes or until the onions are soft and golden.

2. Add your stock. Bring to the boil and simmer for about 30 minutes.

3. Remove, blend, and add a good pinch of salt and pepper.

4. Serve topped with cream and fresh coriander.

Goat's Cheese Salad

Ingredients

- 150 grams mixed greens, preferably rocket or cos lettuce
- 200 grams goat's cheese, sliced and briefly torched or grilled until browned
- Caramelized walnuts (walnuts stir-fried in 50 grams butter and 50 grams sugar for 2 minutes)
- cracked black pepper
- Honey Mustard Dressing (blend 30 grams honey, 3 heaped tablespoons Dijon mustard, and 30 millilitres olive oil)
- caramelized onion (See Irish Sides, Tops, and Stocks)

Method

1. Add your greens to a deep dish.
2. Sprinkle over some cheese, caramelized nuts, pepper, and dressing.
3. Top with caramelized onion. Serve with brown bread.

Smoked Salmon and King Prawn Salad

Ingredients

- 200 grams mixed leaves, preferably rocket or cos lettuce
- 200 grams smoked salmon
- 200 grams king prawns
- Caramelized walnuts (walnuts stir-fried in 50 grams butter and 50 grams sugar for 2 minutes)
- Creamy Balsamic Dressing (blend 2 teaspoons garlic powder, 20 millilitres balsamic vinegar, 30 grams cracked black pepper, honey, and 40 millilitres olive oil)

Method

1. Add your greens to a deep dish. Place some salmon and prawns throughout.
2. Sprinkle over some caramelized nuts, pepper, and dressing.
3. Serve with brown bread.

Salmon Cakes

A real crowd-pleaser. Try them topped with a little caramelized onion.

Ingredients

- butter, for frying
- 4 shallots, peeled and finely chopped
- 5 tablespoons fresh parsley
- 150 millilitres white wine
- 100 millilitres fish stock
- 50 millilitres water
- 4 sprigs fresh thyme
- 500 grams boneless salmon fillets
- 600 grams potatoes, peeled and chopped into small cubes
- 50 millilitres milk
- 80 grams breadcrumbs
- 50 grams flour
- juice of half a lemon
- 1 large egg, beaten
- 1 1/2 tablespoons fresh coriander
- salt and pepper

Directions:

1. Add some butter to a large saucepan over low heat. After a minute, throw in your shallots and parsley. Fry for 2 minutes, stirring frequently.
2. Add your wine, stock, water, and thyme. Bring to the boil and then reduce to a low heat.
3. Add your salmon to the pan – carefully, as you will have to take this out later. Placing it skin-side down helps.
4. Simmer for 12 minutes and then remove the salmon to a warm dish.
5. Add your potatoes to the pan and cook until soft. Meanwhile, use a fork to flake your salmon from the skin.
6. Remove the sprigs of thyme from your pan. Drain and mash the potatoes.
7. With your hands or a standing mixer, combine the mash, flaked salmon, milk, breadcrumbs, flour, lemon juice, egg, coriander, and a good pinch of salt and pepper in a large mixing bowl. Set aside in the fridge to set for at least 20 minutes.
8. Shape the mix into thick disks about the size of the rim of a mug and fry over low heat in some butter until crisp and golden all over.
9. Serve and enjoy!

Crispy Cheese Mushroom Melts

A very easy starter with charm that's always popular at parties.

Ingredients

- 8 portobello mushrooms, cleaned, stalks removed
- 40 grams breadcrumbs
- 1 large egg, beaten
- 1 tablespoon fresh parsley
- 1 teaspoon dried thyme
- 150 grams farmhouse dairy cheese, grated
- salt and pepper
- 8 sun-dried tomatoes

Method

1. Preheat oven to 200 degrees C. Bake your mushrooms on a greased sheet of baking paper or foil for 10 minutes.

2. Meanwhile, mix together your breadcrumbs, egg, parsley, thyme, cheese, and a good pinch of salt and pepper.

3. Reduce heat to 180 degrees C. Top your mushrooms with the breadcrumb mixture and place a sun-dried tomato atop each one. Bake for about 15 minutes.

4. Remove and serve when golden brown and crispy on top.

The Hairy Lem...

Centennial

Key Ring

€3

IRISH TOPS, SIDES, AND STOCKS

Champ Mash

This classic side has a real Irish flavour which will remind any Irish person of home.

Ingredients

- 2 kilograms potatoes, peeled and diced
- 300 millilitres milk
- 250 grams scallions or onions, chopped
- 80 grams butter
- salt and pepper

Method

1. Cook your potatoes in a large pot of boiling water.

2. Meanwhile, add the milk and scallions to a separate saucepan and simmer together for about 5 minutes.

3. When your potatoes are cooked, strain and mash them until smooth. Now add your milk and scallions along with the butter, salt, and pepper. Mix well and serve.

Boxty

This is a lovely crispy golden-fried side that delights the senses with its looks, texture, and flavour. It is ideally cooked on a waffle or sandwich toaster, which also gives it a nice shape and form.

Ingredients

- 500 grams raw peeled then grated potato
- 500 grams mashed potato
- 500 grams plain flour
- salt and pepper
- 50 millilitres milk
- 1 egg, beaten

Method

1. Mix together grated raw potato, mashed potato, flour, salt, and pepper.
2. Add your milk and egg; mix well.
3. Pour the mixture onto a pan in small squares about the size of the rim of a mug. Cook until crisp and golden. Flip over, repeat on the other side, and serve. If you use a sandwich toaster, the cooking will be faster and easier.

Colcannon

This is a famous Irish side bursting with taste and texture. It will satisfy the most ferocious of appetites.

Ingredients

- 500 grams potatoes, peeled
- 450 grams kale or cabbage, chopped to a medium coarseness
- 125 grams onion, scallion, or leek
- 25 grams butter, plus more for sautéing
- 80 millilitres milk
- salt and pepper

Directions

1. Cook your potatoes in a large pot of boiling water.
2. Meanwhile, in a separate pan, cook your kale in boiling water for about 10 minutes.
3. While these two are cooking, sauté your onion in a pan with a little butter for 2 minutes over medium heat.
4. Preheat oven to 160 degrees C. When your potatoes are cooked, strain and mash them thoroughly and add in the strained kale, sautéed onion, butter, milk, and a good pinch of salt and pepper. Mix together well.
5. Place your pot into the oven and bake for 15 to 20 minutes.

Potato Cakes

Also known as potato scallops, this filling Irish side is loved by all. Serve it with a little potato salad.

Ingredients

- 3 large potatoes, peeled and boiled
- 2 teaspoons plain flour
- 2 tablespoons milk
- 20 grams butter, plus more for frying
- salt and pepper

Directions:

1. Mash your potatoes thoroughly and add the flour, milk, butter, salt, and pepper.

2. Mix well and make into thick pancake disks about the width of the rim of a mug. Fry in some butter in a pan on medium heat until golden brown on both sides and cooked through. Serve immediately.

Potato Salad

A creamy soft potato side with delicious crunchy vegetables. A side to have with any other side!

Ingredients

- 500 grams baby potatoes, peeled and boiled
- 3 chopped scallions
- 2 hard-boiled eggs
- 1/2 onion, chopped
- 3 tablespoons malt vinegar
- 2 small pickled gherkins, chopped
- 1 teaspoon mustard
- 150 millilitres mayo

Method

Combine all ingredients in a large mixing bowl and mix well. Refrigerate for at least an hour before serving.

Caramelized Onion

Ingredients

- 1 large onion, peeled and chopped
- 50 grams sugar
- 15 grams butter

Method

1. Add the sugar and butter to a saucepan over a low to medium heat and cook a couple of minutes to form a brownish liquid caramel.
2. Add your onion and toss in the caramel sauce for about a minute.
3. Remove from the pan and serve.

Chicken Stock

This classic stock forms the basis of a great many fine soups and sauces.

Ingredients

- 2 kilograms chicken bones and trimmings
- 6 litres water
- 200 grams carrots, peeled
- 200 grams mushrooms, washed
- 2 onions, peeled
- 2 celery stalks, washed
- 20 white peppercorns
- 2 garlic cloves
- 2 cloves

Method

1. Wash the chicken bones and trimmings under cold running water for several hours.
2. Add the chicken and water to a large pot and bring to the boil. Lower the heat and simmer gently.
3. After 10 minutes, skim any excess fat from the surface and add the remaining ingredients. Simmer for 2 to 3 hours, skimming the excess fat every hour.
4. Strain the stock through a muslin-lined sieve. Allow to cool fully and refrigerate. The stock can be stored for up to 1 week in the fridge or several weeks in the freezer.

Variations

- For beef stock, use beef trimmings and bones instead of chicken.
- For fish stock, use fish bones, heads, and trimmings (preferably turbot, halibut, sole, or brill) instead of the chicken, and use 4 litres water together with 500 millilitres white wine. Simmer the stock for 40 minutes instead of 2 to 3 hours and strain.

Pastry Tops

Ingredients

- 300 grams flour
- 1 teaspoon salt
- 50 grams cold butter
- cold water

Method

1. In a large bowl, mix together the flour and salt. Make a well in the centre.
2. Rub the butter until soft and mix with the flour mixture until it resembles breadcrumbs.
3. Add cold water a spoonful at a time until a relatively stiff dough is formed.
4. Wrap the dough in cling film. Flatten out the top and place in the fridge for about 2 hours.
5. Preheat oven to 180 degrees C. Roll out the dough to an inch thickness on a lightly floured surface and cut into the desired shape to fit your dish. (With any remaining dough, you can make shamrocks to place atop your pastry tops and bake together for a touch of flair.)
6. Pierce the pastry all over with a fork for an even rise and bake for 15 minutes or until crisp and golden.

Serving

- Makes 8

IRISH MAINS

Irish Stew

Ingredients

- butter, for frying
- 1 kilogram diced lamb, preferably shoulder
- 2 chicken stock cubes, divided
- 2 large onions, peeled and roughly chopped
- 1 heaped tablespoon flour
- 3 tablespoons chopped fresh parsley
- 5 sprigs fresh thyme
- 1 heaped tablespoon rosemary
- 400 grams carrots, washed, peeled and chopped into large pieces
- 4 celery stalks, washed and chopped roughly
- 500 grams potatoes, washed, peeled and chopped into large pieces
- salt and pepper

Method

1. Heat some butter in a large frying pan over medium to high heat.
2. Rub the meat with half a stock cube and brown in the pan on all sides. Transfer to a large pot to rest.
3. Reduce the heat in your frying pan to low. Add some more butter and your chopped onion. Allow the onions to cook for 3 or 4 minutes until about to turn golden. Add your flour, stir, and cook for about 45 seconds.
4. Using the remaining 1 1/2 stock cubes, make 1 litre of stock. Add roughly 1/3 to your onion mixture and bring to the boil.
5. Reduce to a simmer and add to your meat in the large pot along with your herbs, remaining stock, carrots, and celery. Cover and simmer for 90 minutes, stirring and removing the fat gathered on the top layer intermittently.
6. Add your potatoes and cook for another 30 to 40 minutes, or until the potatoes are cooked through.
7. Now bring your stew to the boil and ladle out the excess fat from the top over about 5 minutes until it's mostly gone.
8. Reduce heat and remove thyme stalks. Add a good pinch of salt and pepper. Stir and serve with some champ mash and brown bread.

Pastry-Topped Beef 'n' Guinness Pie

Ingredients

- butter, for frying
- 1 kilogram diced beef, preferably shoulder
- 1 chicken stock cube
- 2 large onions, peeled and roughly chopped
- 1 tablespoon flour
- 500 millilitres Guinness stout
- 4 sprigs fresh thyme
- 4 tablespoons fresh parsley
- 2 heaped tablespoons tomato puree
- 1 teaspoon sugar
- 300 grams carrots, washed, peeled and roughly chopped
- 4 celery stalks, washed and roughly chopped
- 500 grams potatoes, washed, peeled and roughly chopped
- salt and pepper
- Pastry Top (See Irish Tops, Sides and Stocks)

Method

1. Heat some butter in a large frying pan over medium to high heat.

2. Rub the meat with half a stock cube and brown in the pan on all sides. Transfer to a large pot to rest.

3. Reduce the heat in your frying pan to low. Add some more butter and your chopped onion. Allow the onions to cook for 3 or 4 minutes until about to turn golden. Add your flour, stir, and cook for about 45 seconds.

4. Add your Guinness and simmer for about 5 minutes.

5. Make 400 millilitres chicken stock with the remaining 1/2 stock cube. Add the Guinness mixture and stock to your meat in the large pot along with your herbs, tomato puree, sugar, carrots, and celery. Cover and simmer over a low heat for 90 minutes, stirring and skimming the top layer of fat intermittently.

6. Add your potatoes and cook for another 30 to 40 minutes, or until the potatoes are cooked through.

7. Remove your stalks of thyme. Add a good pinch of salt and pepper. Serve in a bowl with a Pastry Top and some soda bread on the side.

Dublin Coddle

Ingredients

- butter, for frying
- 400 grams carrots, peeled and roughly chopped
- 4 celery stalks, washed and roughly chopped
- 2 large onions, peeled and roughly chopped
- 4 tablespoons chopped fresh parsley
- 500 grams bacon slices, cut into strips
- 500 grams good pork sausages
- 1 litre chicken stock (See Irish Tops, Sides, and Stocks)
- 500 grams potatoes, peeled and roughly chopped
- salt and freshly ground pepper

Method

1. Add some butter to a large pot over a low heat. Add your carrots, celery, onions, and parsley. Stir frequently over 5 minutes.
2. Add your bacon, sausages, and stock. Bring to the boil.
3. Reduce to a simmer. Cover and cook for 1 hour, stirring and removing the top layer of fat intermittently.
4. Add your potatoes and cook for another 30 to 40 minutes.
5. Bring to the boil and remove any excess fat over a couple of minutes.
6. Season with salt and pepper to taste.
7. Serve hot in a bowl with some brown bread and colcannon on the side.

Bacon-Wrapped Breast of Chicken with Goat's Cheese, Caramelized Onion, and Champ Mash

Ingredients

- 4 bacon slices
- butter, for frying
- 4 chicken breast fillets
- 1 tablespoon chopped fresh parsley
- 6 garlic cloves, crushed
- 200 grams goat's cheese
- champ mash (See Irish Sides, Tops, and Stocks)
- mixed salad, for garnish
- caramelized onion (See Irish Sides, Tops, and Stocks)

Method

1. Fry your bacon in a little butter over a medium heat in a saucepan. Remove bacon to one side when cooked but retain the fat in the pan.

2. Add your chicken fillets, parsley, and garlic. Stir until your chicken is cooked through.

3. Remove your fillets and wrap with the bacon slices.

4. Top the fillets with goat's cheese and torch or grill until the cheese is lightly browned.

5. Serve on a bed of champ mash with a small mixed salad on the side. Place some caramelized onion on top of your goat's cheese and enjoy.

Bacon-Wrapped Bangers with Caramelized Onion and Champ Mash

Ingredients

- butter for frying
- 8 large good pork sausages
- 8 bacon slices
- salt and pepper
- champ mash (See Irish Sides, Tops, and Stocks)
- caramelized onion (See Irish Sides, Tops, and Stocks)

Method

1. Heat some butter over a medium heat in a frying pan and quickly brown your sausages and bacon for about 2 minutes.
2. Remove from the heat and wrap the bacon around the sausages. Grill on a medium heat for 5 minutes, turning halfway.
3. Remove when the bacon is crisp.
4. Season with salt and pepper to taste.
5. Serve on a bed of champ mash.
6. For added flair, pour some gravy around your mash and top the meat with caramelized onion.

Guinness-Braised Lamb Shanks

The most flavoursome lamb meat cooked until tender in a dish widely praised by all.

Ingredients

- 4 lamb shanks
- salt and pepper
- butter, for frying
- 3 celery stalks, washed chopped
- 2 carrots, washed, peeled and chopped
- 1 large onion, washed, peeled and chopped
- 1 heaped tablespoon tomato puree
- 400 millilitres Guinness stout
- 500 millilitres vegetable stock
- 6 garlic cloves, peeled and split in two
- 6 sprigs fresh rosemary
- 3 tablespoons fresh thyme
- 3 tablespoons balsamic vinegar
- Caramelized onion (See Irish Sides, Tops, and Stocks)

Method

1. Season the lamb with a good amount of salt and pepper and rub into the meat.

2. Add butter to a large saucepan over a medium heat and brown the lamb shanks on all sides. Remove from the heat and set aside in a large baking dish.

3. Add the celery, carrots, and onion to your pan over a medium heat with some more butter and cook, stirring frequently, for several minutes or until the onion becomes translucent.

4. Stir in the tomato puree and immediately deglaze by adding the Guinness. Bring to a boil and then simmer for 5 minutes. Preheat the oven to 160 degrees C.

5. Add the stock, garlic, rosemary, thyme, and balsamic vinegar. Bring to a simmer.

6. Carefully add this mixture to your lamb in the baking dish. Cover the dish loosely with foil and cook in the oven for 2 1/2 hours, skimming any excess fat every hour.

7. Remove the shanks and set aside. Pour the remaining sauce back into a saucepan and reduce over a high heat for 5 to 10 minutes.

8. Place a lamb shank over a bed of champ mash and dress with some of the sauce. Top with some caramelized onion and enjoy.

Bacon and Cabbage

An Irish favourite at any table. This dish has the finest tender meat textures and a delicious refined bacon flavour.

Ingredients

- 1 shoulder of bacon, boned and rolled
- 1 large carrot
- 1 leek
- 2 celery stalks
- 3 bay leaves
- 2 small onions, divided
- 1 head cabbage, cored and chopped
- butter, for frying
- 50 grams flour
- 150 millilitres milk
- 100 millilitres white wine
- 3 tablespoons fresh parsley
- 2 tablespoons chopped fresh chives
- 4 garlic cloves
- champ mash (See Irish Tops, Sides, and Stocks)

Method

1. Soak your shoulder of bacon overnight in water, with the water changed several times, to reduce the saltiness of the meat before cooking.

2. Make a mirepoix to flavour the meat by chopping the carrot, leek, celery, bay leaves, and one of the onions.

3. Add the mirepoix along with the bacon to a large pot and cover with water a couple of inches above the meat. Bring to a simmer and cook for 35 minutes per kilo. When this time has elapsed, remove the pot from the heat and leave for 25 minutes. Remove the meat from the pot, place on a warm dish, and cover with cling film to retain the heat. Allow to rest while preparing the remainder of the dish.

4. Add your cabbage to the pot and cook over a low heat for about 10 minutes in the bacon water.

5. For your sauce, chop your remaining onion thinly and cook it in a pan in some butter over a medium heat. When the onion becomes translucent, add the flour and stir for 1 minute. Add 250 millilitres of the bacon water along with the milk, wine, and parsley. Simmer for 5 minutes, stirring frequently. Add the chives and set aside.

6. Carve your meat into thick slices. Plate and serve with your cabbage, sauce, and some champ mash and enjoy.

Beer-Battered Fish and Twice-Fried Chips

Ingredients

- vegetable oil, for deep frying
- 1 kilogram potatoes, peeled and chopped into chips, and then left to soak in water for at least 20 minutes
- 100 grams flour
- 1 egg
- salt and pepper
- 200 millilitres lager
- 4 cod fillets
- malt vinegar

Method

1. Heat the oil to 165 degrees C. Pat your potatoes dry with a clean cloth and carefully add to the oil. Cook for about 5 minutes and remove to a dish.

2. Meanwhile, make your batter by adding your flour to a bowl with the egg and a good sprinkle of salt and pepper. Mix in the lager. Set aside until later.

3. Bring your oil up to 185 degrees C. Coat your fish in the batter and carefully add to the hot oil. Cook for about 5 minutes or until crisp and light golden brown. Remove to a dish with some paper towels to absorb any excess oil.

4. Add your once-fried chips back to the oil and cook again until golden brown (or several minutes more, depending on the size of your chips). Remove to a dish lined with a paper towel.

5. Plate side by side with a ramekin of hot marrowfat peas and a ramekin of tartar sauce. Sprinkle generously with malt vinegar and salt before serving.

Crusted Lamb Roast

Ingredients

- 350 grams breadcrumbs
- 4 tablespoons chopped fresh parsley
- 50 grams butter
- salt and pepper
- 1 shoulder of lamb (1.8 kilograms)
- 700 grams potatoes, washed, peeled, and chopped roughly
- 4 sprigs fresh thyme
- 3 sprigs rosemary
- 2 large onions
- 12 baby carrots, lightly scrubbed
- 6 baby turnip, washed and peeled
- 2 medium apples
- 400 millilitres chicken stock

Method

1. Preheat the oven to 200 degrees C.
2. In a bowl, mix the breadcrumbs, parsley, butter, and a good pinch of salt and pepper together into a paste.
3. Score the meat all over with a sharp knife and rub the paste all over the meat, pressing it and forming a crumb all over.
4. In a large baking dish, add all remaining ingredients, starting with the potatoes and finishing by placing the meat on top.
5. Cover loosely with foil and bake for 45 minutes.
6. Lower heat to 180 degrees C and cook for another 90 minutes.
7. Remove the foil and bake for 30 more minutes or until a rich brown crust has formed. Serve and enjoy.

Variations

- Add 6 shallots, unsliced.
- Replace 200 millilitres of the stock with white wine.

Cottage Pie

A tasty and warming ever popular classic dish which never fails to satisfy.

Ingredients:

- 850 g Potatoes, peeled and chopped into halves.
- 50g Butter, for mash.
- 50ml Whole milk.
- Butter for frying.
- 1 Medium Onion, finely chopped.
- 2 Sticks of Celery, finely chopped.
- 1 large Carrot, peeled and finely chopped.
- 2 Garlic cloves, crushed.
- 1KG Minced Beef.
- 2 Tblspn Tomato Puree.
- 2Tp of Worcester sauce
- 100ml Beef Stock (or Guinness for an Irish twist.)
- 200g Dubliner Cheddar cheese or another good red cheddar, grated.
- Salt and Pepper.

Method

Add the potatoes to a large pot. Cover with cold water and sprinkle in a good pinch of salt. Bring to the boil and simmer for 20 minutes or until soft through. (Check by piercing with a knife.) When ready, drain out the water and add the milk and butter and make a smooth mash with a potato masher or your preferred method.

In the meantime, add some butter to a good sized medium hot pan. Add the garlic, onion, celery and carrot to the pan in quick succession and sauté for 4 to 5 minutes or until starting to soften, stirring regularly.

Add the minced beef to the pan and brown, stirring and breaking up the meat.

Lower the heat and add the tomato puree, a good pinch of salt, pepper, worchester and stock or Guinness and allow to cook for another 10 minutes.

Preheat your oven to 180C. Transfer the meat mixture into a large ovenproof casserole dish or 5 to 6 smaller individual ones. Cover the meat with the mashed potato and make flick marks on the top using a fork. Sprinkle the cheese on top and cook in the oven for 15 minutes or until the top looks crispy and golden.

Serve immediately with a slice of buttered home-made brown bread and accept the praise graciously.

DESSERTS

Apple Cake with Paddy Irish Whiskey Custard

This popular classic always pleases, and with the delicious warming Paddy Whiskey Custard, you will have the table praising you with mmmms and oohs!

Ingredients

- 130 grams plain flour
- 1/2 teaspoon salt
- 1/2 teaspoon baking soda
- 1/2 teaspoon nutmeg
- 1/2 teaspoon baking powder
- 60 grams unsalted butter
- 130 grams granulated sugar
- 1 egg
- 1 teaspoon vanilla essence
- 4 large cooking apples, preferably tangy Granny Smiths, peeled, cored, and diced into small chunks
- Paddy Irish Whiskey Custard (see recipe at end of chapter)

Method

1. Preheat oven to 180 degrees C. In a large bowl, sift together the flour, salt, soda, nutmeg, and baking powder.

2. In another large bowl, mix together the butter and sugar with a hand mixer until creamy, and then beat in the egg until the mixture is light and fluffy.

3. Gradually add the flour mixture to the egg mixture until well incorporated. Mix in the vanilla and then the apples.

4. Pour the batter into a well greased 10-inch springform cake tin. Bake for about 40 minutes or until a knife inserted into the middle of the cake comes out clean.

5. Release the springform-tin sides to aid the cooling process. Allow at least 20 minutes to cool.

6. Pour the custard over the top and serve.

Nana Bacon's Best-Ever Bread and Butter Pudding with Apricot and Paddy Irish Whiskey Custard

This famous classic is all too often undervalued due to various poor versions. Ours is a more refined adaptation which uses a pastry-like brioche to earn this dessert the credit it deserves.

Ingredients

- 800 millilitres cream
- 2 vanilla pods, sliced and scraped
- 2 teaspoons vanilla essence
- 7 egg yolks
- 200 grams caster sugar, divided
- 4 packets brioche (1200 grams)
- butter
- apricot jam
- 100 grams sultanas
- 1/2 sliced pan
- Paddy Irish Whiskey Custard (see recipe at end of chapter)

Method

1. Bring your cream to a simmer along with your vanilla pods and essence in a large pot. When it reaches a simmer, remove from the heat and allow to settle for 15 minutes.

2. In a bowl, blanch your egg yolks by whisking in 200 grams of the caster sugar until combined.

3. Take some of the cream mixture from the pot and mix together rapidly with the yolk mixture so as not to cook the eggs. Add this mixture back to the pot of cream over a medium heat, stirring frequently until a thick custard is formed (about 3 minutes).

4. Slice your brioche lengthways into halves. Layer a casserole dish, first spreading the bottom halves with butter and the top halves with apricot jam, leaving enough pieces spare to make to top layer of the pudding.

5. Pour half of the custard over the brioche and sprinkle with the sultanas.

6. Remove the crusts from the sliced pan and make another layer in the pudding. Pour some more custard over.

7. Make a top layer for the pudding with the remaining brioche and pour over the remaining custard. Let stand for 15 minutes to allow the bread to absorb the creamy custard. Preheat the oven to 140 degrees C.

8. Cover the pudding with foil and bake in the oven for 30 minutes.

9. Remove foil and bake for 10 more minutes, or until a golden crust has formed. Grill carefully for 1 or 2 minutes if necessary.

10. Serve hot, topped with the custard.

Guinness Chocolate Velvet Cake

This modern Irish cake has appeal on so many levels. The magical combination of chocolate and stout creates an unmistakably rich and smooth new flavour – especially enticing for chocoholics who love a pint.

Ingredients

- 400 millilitres Guinness Irish stout
- 100 grams natural cocoa powder
- 150 grams cooking chocolate (minimum 60 per cent cocoa solids), grated finely
- 230 grams plain flour
- 1 teaspoon baking soda
- 1/2 teaspoon baking powder
- 220 grams unsalted butter
- 350 grams granulated sugar
- 4 eggs

Method

1. Pour the Guinness into a large bowl and then add the cocoa. Mix well. Add the grated chocolate and set aside.

2. In another bowl, sift together the flour, baking soda, and baking powder.

3. Soften the butter by leaving out or microwave on a defrost heat for a minute. In yet another large bowl, whisk together the butter with the sugar until creamy. Beat the eggs into the butter mixture one at a time.

4. Gradually add the flour mixture to the egg mixture until well incorporated. Gradually add the Guinness mixture and blend well.

5. Scoop the batter into a 12-inch springform baking tin and bake at 180 degrees Celsius for 60 to 70 minutes, or until a knife inserted into the centre of the cake comes out clean.

6. Remove from the oven and release the springform-tin sides to aid cooling. Serve with ice cream or whipped cream.

Chocolate Orange Tart

This ethereal and dangerously charming treat will impress the most sophisticated and bring anyone to their knees for the chance to beg for more.

Ingredients

Pastry

- 180 grams plain flour
- 30 grams natural cocoa powder
- 30 grams icing sugar
- 1/2 teaspoon salt
- 120 grams unsalted butter
- 1 egg yolk
- 40 millilitres cold water

Tart

- 80 grams baking chocolate (minimum 60 per cent cocoa solids), grated finely
- 2 large oranges
- 150 grams caster sugar
- 4 eggs
- 150 millilitres double cream
- icing sugar for dusting

Method

Pastry

1. In a large bowl, sift together the flour, cocoa, sugar, and salt.
2. Add the butter and mix until well incorporated.
3. Add the egg yolk and then the water. Mix well.
4. Fold into a lump. Wrap with cling film and chill for 40 minutes.
5. Roll out the pastry evenly onto the base of a well-greased 9-inch springform cake tin and chill for 90 minutes.

Tart

1. Preheat oven to 200 degrees C.
2. Place the pastry in the oven and bake for 15 minutes. Watch the time with this one, as this chocolate pastry will become bitter if overdone.
3. As soon as you remove it from the oven, sprinkle the hot pastry evenly with the grated chocolate. Set aside. Reduce oven temperature to 160 degrees C.
4. Grate the orange zest into a large bowl. Add the sugar and the juice from the oranges. Mix well.
5. Whisk in the eggs and then the cream until well incorporated. Pour over the pastry in the springform tin and bake for about 30 minutes or until set.
6. Release the springform-tin sides to aid cooling. Allow to cool completely. Dust with sugar and serve.

Connemara Peated Whiskey Cake with Whiskey Icing

This delicious classic Irish dessert has a lovely warmth and takes most diners back to their youth with the feel of sitting around Granny's table – but don't tell Dad what happened to his bottle of whiskey!

Ingredients

Cake

- 130 grams plain flour
- 1 teaspoon nutmeg
- 1/2 teaspoon baking soda
- 1/2 teaspoon baking powder
- 1/2 teaspoon salt
- 120 grams unsalted butter
- 1 1/4 cups icing sugar
- 3 eggs
- 3/4 cup Connemara peated Irish whiskey
- juice of 1 lemon
- 2 cups walnuts (100 grams to be crushed before addition)
- 2 cups sultanas (100 grams)

Icing

- 1 cup icing sugar
- 70 grams unsalted butter
- 1/2 cup Connemara peated Irish whiskey

Method

Cake

1. In a large bowl, sift together the flour, nutmeg, baking soda, baking powder, and salt.
2. In a separate bowl, beat together the butter and sugar until creamy.
3. Add the eggs to the butter and sugar. Mix well until fluffy.
4. Add the flour mixture gradually until well incorporated.
5. Add the whiskey and the lemon juice to the mixture. Blend together well.
6. Preheat oven to 180 degrees C. Blend the nuts and fruit into the batter and pour into a 12-inch springform baking tin. Bake for about 30 to 35 minutes, or until a knife inserted into the centre of the cake comes out clean. When the cake is ready, release the springform-tin sides, as this will aid the cooling process.

Icing

1. Mix the sugar and butter in a bowl until smooth.
2. Gradually add the whiskey until well incorporated.
3. When the cake has cooled, apply the icing to the top and sides. Chill to set.

Baileys Irish Cream and Strawberry Fool

This refreshing, light, and simple dessert tantalizes the eyes – and *with the unique Baileys Irish Cream warmth and flavour, it's sure to bring a round of smiles and liven up any party.*

Ingredients

- 400 millilitres double cream
- 500 grams fresh strawberries, washed, husks removed
- 120 millilitres Baileys Irish Cream Liqueur
- 2 teaspoons icing sugar

Preparation

This dessert is best served in chilled glasses and will serve six, so before you start, place six glasses (preferably stemmed) into the refrigerator.

Method

1. Using an electric mixer, whip the cream until stiff.
2. Set aside 6 strawberries for topping. Puree the rest.
3. Add the Baileys Irish Cream and half the strawberry puree to the whipped cream. Blend together well.
4. Carefully spoon some of the strawberry puree into each glass, followed by the Baileys Irish Cream mixture. Repeat to form layers.
5. Dust each serving with a little icing sugar and place a strawberry atop each one. Enjoy (the dessert and the praise)!

Created by Angela & Melissa Cooper & unique to the hairy lemon cafe bar.

Guinness Chocolate Mousse

This luxurious chocolate mousse is irresistible to the taste and the eye. It is supposed to look like a glass of Guinness and it is the source of much fame and praise.

This recipe was created by Melissa and Angela Cooper and is unique to The Hairy Lemon Restaurant.

Ingredients

- 160 grams dark chocolate (minimum 60 per cent cocoa solids), broken into small pieces
- 160 grams icing sugar
- 4 large eggs, separated
- 60 grams cocoa powder
- 100 millilitres whipping cream
- 80 millilitres Guinness stout
- 50 grams digestive biscuits

Method

- Melt the chocolate in a large heatproof bowl over a saucepan of barely simmering water and remove from the heat.
- Stir in the icing sugar. Add the egg yolks one at a time, and then add the cocoa.
- In a bowl, whisk the egg whites until stiff peaks form.
- In another bowl, whip the cream until thick. Portion some away to top your mousse at the final stage.
- Alternating, mix some of the egg whites and then the cream into the chocolate mixture until combined. Be careful not to over-mix.
- Pour your mousse into glasses, leaving enough room for a thin layer of biscuit and a cream head. (A Guinness glass makes a big difference.)
- Crush the biscuits and sprinkle a layer over the mousse. Allow to set in the fridge for several hours.
- Top with whipped cream for the Guinness look and enjoy.

Paddy Irish Whiskey Custard

Ingredients

- 300 millilitres milk
- 300 millilitres double cream
- 1 teaspoon vanilla essence
- 4 egg yolks
- 100 grams granulated sugar
- 80 millilitres Paddy Irish whiskey

Method

1. Pour the milk and cream into a medium-sized pan and bring to the boil over a low to medium heat. Immediately remove from the heat, as the mixture will quickly burn otherwise.

2. In the meantime, whisk together the vanilla essence, egg yolks, and sugar until light and fluffy. Add the cream mixture to the egg mixture and blend well.

3. Return to the heat and cook until the mixture is thick and coats the back of a dipped spoon.

4. Add your whiskey. Stir well, pour over your cake, and enjoy.

DRINKS

Whiskey Sour

1 measure Paddy Irish whiskey

1 mixer lemon bitters

Mix and serve on ice.

The Orange Man

1 measure Paddy Irish whiskey

1 mixer ginger ale

1 mixer orange soda

Serve together over ice.

Lime Ginger Whiskey

1 measure Paddy Irish whiskey

1 mixer ginger ale

slice of lime

Pour together on ice and serve.

Minted Whiskey

1 measure Paddy Irish whiskey

1 measure crème de menthe

fresh mint

Mix together in a shaker and serve in a chilled stemmed glass.

Irish Mind Explosion

300 millilitres Guinness Irish stout

1 measure Paddy Irish whiskey

1 measure Baileys Irish Cream liqueur

Pour the Guinness into a large glass. Allow to settle before adding the remaining ingredients. Allow this concoction to settle again and drink. (This is meant to be downed in one. Use your own discretion.)

Black Velvet

125ml Chilled Guinness or another stout

125ml Chilled Champagne or sparkling white
wine.

There is another version of this which uses
cider instead of wine which is also a great
long drink.

Tilt the glass and pour the Guinness in slowly.
Allow to settle and again tilt the glass and
slowly add the champagne. Serve and enjoy.

Hot Toddy

This is a classic Irish winter warmer and is often used medicinally to help shake off a cold or flu.

1 Teaspoon sugar

1 Measure of Powers Gold Label Irish whiskey or your preferred whiskey.

100ml hot water

A slice of lemon.

2 Cloves.

Add the hot water and sugar to a glass and stir until dissolved. Add the whiskey, cloves and lemon and stir. Serve hot.

Hot Toddy

Old Fashioned

2 Measures Powers Gold Label whiskey or your preferred whiskey.

1 Measure Gomme sugar syrup. (Make by adding equal parts sugar and hot water. Stir until dissolved and allow to cool.)

Some thin slices of orange peel.

Add some ice, the whiskey and sugar syrup to a shaker. Thinly slice the very outer skin from an orange being careful not to add any of the white rind. Add several slices to the shaker and shake well for 10 seconds. Use some of the orange peel to rub the orange oil on the inside of the skin on the rim of a glass. Add ice to the glass. Strain and serve. Top with 2 or 3 twists of the orange peel.

Old fashioned

Hair of the Dog

This old expression is a way of saying that the best way to feel better after too many drinks the night before is to have another drink.

1 Measure of Powers Gold Label Whiskey (or your preferred whiskey)

1 and ½ Measures cream

½ Measure honey

Add ice and all ingredients to a shaker. Shake for 10 seconds, strain into a cocktail glass and serve.

Hair of the dog

Irish Coffee

Ingredients

- 1 teaspoon sugar
- 120 millilitres coffee, preferably made using a good ground coffee bean
- 1 measure Paddy Irish whiskey
- 40 millilitres whipped cream

Method

Add the sugar to the coffee and stir in. Add the whiskey and then gently spoon the whipped cream over the top to form a head. Serve immediately.

Irish coffee

Baileys Coffee

Ingredients

- 1 teaspoon sugar
- 120 millilitres coffee, preferably made using a good ground coffee bean
- 1 measure Baileys Irish Cream liqueur
- 40 millilitres whipped cream

Method

Add the sugar to the coffee and stir in. Add the liqueur and gently spoon the whipped cream over the top to form a head. Serve immediately.

The Chefs

Andrea and Julian

Drinking Tips

Whiskey is an old Irish spirit. The word actually comes from the Gaelic (Irish) word for water which is *uisce*, from the phrase *uisce beathe* – "water of life."

Irish whiskey is enjoyed by connoisseurs on many levels, unlike most other spirits. From the sound of its drop into the glass (believe it or not, a bulbed whiskey glass makes a considerable difference on several levels) to its aroma, body, warmth, and character, it has a refined complexity that has to be experienced to be understood.

When poured a measure, it's best to inhale the aroma deeply into your nostrils first and follow with a small sip. Allow this to sit on your tongue for a prolonged moment. This seems to create a kind of base in the mouth, which will improve the flavour of the rest of the measure.

Guinness Irish stout is another wonderful Irish drink. It was created when the hops and barley in a recipe for beer were reversed, to astonishing effect. The drink actually has remarkable health benefits. For over sixty years, the company's advertising campaign was that Guinness is good for you and has been recommended by doctors. Stout was actually prescribed to blood donors, who received a half pint after a donation. This guaranteed that the supply of blood donations in Ireland never ran short. It was also recommended to pregnant women, as it is relatively low in alcohol and is bursting with iron, and so acts as an elixir. Also, the yeast aided the birthing.

Another interesting fact about Guinness Irish stout is that regular consumption of carbonated drinks will cause kidney stones over time. Guinness is nitrogenated instead of carbonated. Regular consumption of Guinness Irish stout will actually cure kidney stones. It's the luck o' the Irish!

Beer is made from hops which is a plant. That makes it a vegetable...

THEREFORE, BEER IS A SALAD!

Connemara Whiskey

Connemara Peated Single Malt Irish Whiskey and
Connemara Cask Strength Peated Single Malt Irish Whiskey (58.5%)

Connemara whiskey is a single-malt whiskey of Cooley Distillery, County Louth, Ireland. It is named for the remote region of Connemara.

Unlike other Irish Whiskey malted barley which is about one in Connemara Whiskey as in the Scotch whiskey peat-fire kilned. The malt takes over the Torfbrand a smoke spicy note. In addition, this whiskey – in contrast to traditional Irish whiskey – is distilled not three times, but only twice. It is made with a still that has a slimmer body and longer neck. Only malt from Irish barley is used. The sand-filtered water comes from a reservoir in the Cooley Mountains. In Germany and Austria, Connemara is distributed by Borco-Marken-Import GmbH.

Humorous Irish Sayings, with Translation

"San áit ina mbíonn mná bíonn gab!"
San áit ina mbíonn toit bíonn tine, San áit ina mbíonn tine bíonn teas,
San áit ina mbíonn teas bíonn mná, San áit ina mbíonn mná bíonn gab!
Where there's a roof, there's a fire; where there's a fire, there's heat;
where there's heat, there's women; where there's women, there's gossip!

***

An áit a mbíonn mná bíonn caint agus an áit a mbíonn géanna bíonn callán.
Where there are women there is talk,
and where there are geese there is cackling.

***

Ná bíodh do theanga faoi do chrios.
Don't keep your tongue under your belt.
(Say what you want to say.)

***

Beagán a rá agus é a rá go maith.
Say little, but say it well.

***

An té is mó a osclaíonn a bhéal is é is lú a osclaíonn a sparán.
The one who opens his mouth the most, it is he who opens his purse the least. (Often used in a pub setting for someone who is talking a lot and not buying a round of drinks – a mortal sin in Ireland!)

***

Mórán cainte ar bheagán cúise.
Much talk with little reason.

***

Is binn béal ina thost.
A silent mouth is sweet.

***

Níl aon tóin tinn mar do thóin tinn féin.
There's no sore ass like your own sore ass. (This funny saying is really a play on the famous irish saying *"Níl aon tinteán mar do thinteán féin,"* which means, "There's no place like home.")

***

Muna bhfuil agat ach pocán gabhair, bí i lár an aonaigh leis.
If you only have a buck-goat, be in the middle of the fair with it.
(Whatever talents/assets you have, use them.)
***

Ná feic a bhfeicir, Is ná clois a gcloisir
Is má fiafraítear díot, Abair ná feadrais.
Don't see what you see, don't hear what you hear,
and if you're asked, say you don't know.
(Means "Whatever you say, say nothing!")
***

Is minic a bheir dall ar ghiorria.
It is often a blind person caught a hare. (If someone's bragging about something, this
is a funny Irish saying or put-down along the lines of, "So what's the big deal?")
***

Is fearr marcaíocht ar ghabhair ná siúlóid, dá fheabhas.
A ride, even on a goat, is better by far than having to walk.
***

An té nach bhfuil láidir, ní foláir dó bheith in ann rith go tapa.
He who's not strong has to be able to run well. (Really a play on another
famous Irish saying "*An té nach bhfuil láidir, ní foláir dó bheith glic,*" which
means, "He who is not strong must be clever/cunning.")
***

An tae nach bhfuil láidir, ní foláir dó bheith te.
The tea which is not strong has to be hot.
(No great meaning here, just another humorous play
on the saying "*An té nach bhfuil láidir, ní foláir dó bheith glic.*")
***

Is trom an t-ualach an leisce.
Laziness is a heavy burden.
(Used when you don't feel like doing anything).
***

Níor bhris focal maith fiacail riamh.
A good word never broke a tooth.
***

An t-uan ag múineadh méilí dá mháthair.

The lamb teaching its mother how to bleat.
(A put-down for an uppity child or a bullied parent.)
***

Go gcoinní Dia i mbois a láimhe thú, agus nár dhúna sé a dhorn go teann choíche.
May the Lord keep you in his hand and never close his fist too tight.
***

An té a dtéann teist na mochóirí amach air ní cás dó codladh go headra.
The person who gains the reputation of getting up early can sleep late.
***

Ar mhaithe leis féin a níos an cat crónán.
The cat purrs to please itself.
***

Galar gan náire an tart.
Thirst is a shameless disease.
(Said when you're in need of a drink.)
***

Is fearr a bheith díomhaoin ná droch-ghnóthach.
Better to be idle than up to no good.
(Used when apologizing for doing nothing.)
***

Is geal leis an bhfiach dubh a ghearrcach féin.
The black raven thinks its own offspring is bright.
(Often used as a put-down for a woman bragging about her children.)
***

Ná nocht d'fhiacla go bhféadair an greim do bhreith.
Don't bare your teeth until you can bite.
(Don't threaten if you can't follow through.)
***

Is maith an t-iománaí an té a bhíonn ar an gclaí.
The hurler on the ditch is a great fellow.
(A put-down for the armchair expert.)
***

Nuair a bheidh do lámh i mbéal na con tarraing go réidh í.
When your hand is in the hound's mouth, withdraw it gently.
(Be careful when dealing with somebody powerful.)

***

Baineann an druncaeir an díon dá thigh féin agus cuireann ar thigh an tábhairne é.
The drunkard takes the roof from his own house and puts it on the publican's house.
(The drunk ends up giving everything to the pub owner.)

***

Tuigeann Tadhg Taidhgín.
Big Tadhg understands little Tadhg. (Like understands like.)

***

Go n-ithe an cat thú is go n-ithe an diabhal an cat.
May the cat eat you and the devil eat the cat.
(More of a curse than anything.)

***

Seachain tigh an tabhairne nó is bairnigh is beatha duit
Beware of the drinking house or you'll be living on barnacles.
(If you spend all your time in the pub, you will be penniless.)

***

Na ceithre rud is measa amú:
ceann tinn, béal seirbh, intinn bhuartha, agus poca folamh.
The four least useful things:
a headache, a bitter mouth, a worried mind, and an empty pocket.

***

The Irish are very fair people; they never speak well for one another.

***

As you slide down the banister of life,
may the splinters never point in the wrong direction.

***

Only Irish coffee provides all main essential food groups:
alcohol, caffeine, sugar, and fat.

***

Is minic a bhris béal duine a shrón.
Many a time a man's mouth broke his nose.
Is minic a ghearr teanga duine a scornach.
It is often a person's tongue cuts his throat.
(Both these sayings mean that what you say
can get you into a lot of trouble.)

***

Cuir síoda ar ghabhar ach is gabhar i gcónaí é.
Dress a goat in silk and he still remains a goat.
(You can dress things up or use nice language about something,
but that doesn't hide the reality.)
***

Ní chaitheann an chaint an t-éadach.
Talk doesn't wear the clothes.
(Talk doesn't get the work done.)
***

Ní scéal rúin é ó tá a fhios ag triúr é.
It is not a secret after three people know it.
***

Nuair a bhíonn an cat amuigh, bíonn an luch ag rince.
When the cat is outside, the mouse does the dancing.
(When the cat's away, the mice will play.)
***

Bíonn gach duine go lách go dtéann bó ina gharraí.
Everybody is good natured until a cow goes into his garden.
(Everybody is unconcerned about a matter until affected by it personally.)
***

Inis do Mháire i gcógar é, is inseoidh Máire dó phóbal é.
Tell it to Mary in a whisper, and Mary will tell it to the parish.
(Women like to gossip.)
***

Is teann gach madra gearr i ndoras a thí féin.
Every terrier is bold in the door of its house.
(People can be full of brave talk when near home,
but not so confident when out of their comfort zone.)
***

Glaonn gach coileach go dána ar a atrainn fhéin.
Every cock crows boldly in his own farmyard. (Similar to above.)

Funny Irish Sayings about Love, with Translation

Níl leigheas ar an ngrá ach pósadh.
There is no cure for love other than marriage.
***

Má tá moladh uait, faigh bás; má tá cáineadh uait, pós.
If you want praise, die; if you would complaints, marry.
***

Más mian leat cáineadh pós, Más mian leat moladh faigh bás.
If it's abuse you want, marry. If it's praise you want, die.
***

Pós bean ón sliabh agus pósfaidh tú an sliabh ar fad.
Marry a woman from the mountain, and you will marry the entire mountain.
***

Trí ní is deacair a thuiscint:
intleacht na mban, obair na mbeach,
teacht agus imeacht na taoide.
Three things hardest to understand:
the intellect of women, the work of the bees,
the coming and going of the tide.
***

Má tá tú chun pósadh, pós anuraidh
If you are going to marry, marry last year.
(If you are going to marry, don't leave it too late.)
***

Is minic a chealg briathra míne cailín críonna.
Many a prudent girl was led astray with sweet words.
***

Is maith an bhean í ach níor bhain sí a broga di go foill.
She is a good wife, but she has not taken off her shoes yet.
(Remark about the new wife who hasn't proven herself yet.)
***

Ní féasta go rósta, ní céasadh go pósta
There is no feast without a roast, there is no torment without being married.
(Being married is not always easy.)
***

Is folamh fuar é teach gan bean.
A house without a woman is empty and cold.
***

Is fearr an t-imreas ná an t-uaigneas.
Arguing is better than loneliness.
(We'll put up with a lot to avoid being alone)
***

Faigh do bhean i gcóngar, ach i bhfad uait díol do bhó
Get your wife locally, but far from where you sell your cow. (When you get a wife, better to
know her well, but if you're selling a cow, do it at a distance so there's no comeback.)
***

Faigheann an tseanbhróg an tseanstoca.
The old shoe gets the old stocking.
(For everyone there's someone out there.)
*****

A son is a son till he takes him a wife,
a daughter is a daughter all of her life.

Funny Irish Sayings and Quotes

You've got to do your own growing, no matter how tall your grandfather was.

If you're lucky enough to be Irish, then you're lucky enough.

May the cat eat you and the devil eat the cat.

Who gossips with you will gossip of you.

A good laugh and a long sleep are the two best cures.

But the greatest love – the love above all loves, even greater than that of a mother – is the tender, passionate, undying love of one beer-drunken slob for another.

Don't give cherries to pigs or advice to fools.

The Irish – be they kings, or poets, or farmers – they're a people of great worth; they keep company with the angels and bring a bit of heaven here to earth.

Both your friend and your enemy think you will never die.

Being Irish is very much a part of who I am. I take it everywhere with me.

Why should you never iron a four-leaf clover? You don't want to press your luck.

The Irish gave the bagpipes to the Scots as a joke, but the Scots haven't seen the joke yet.

A turkey never voted for an early Christmas.

Here's to our wives and girlfriends. May they never meet!

The Irish don't know what they want and are prepared to fight to the death to get it.

A quarrel is like buttermilk: once it's out of the churn, the more you shake it, the more sour it grows.

In heaven there is no beer. That's why we drink ours here.

God invented whiskey to keep the Irish from ruling the world.

Drink is the curse of the land. It makes you fight with your neighbour. It makes you shoot at your landlord, and it makes you miss him.

I wouldn't be here if it wasn't for my Mum. I know I've got Irish blood because I wake up every day with a hangover.

It is not a secret after three people know it.

For every wound, a balm. For every sorrow, cheer. For every storm, a calm. For every thirst, a beer.

Bless your little Irish heart and every other Irish part.

When we drink, we get drunk. When we get drunk, we fall asleep. When we fall asleep, we commit no sin. When we commit no sin, we go to heaven. So, let's all get drunk and go to heaven.

Wherever you go and whatever you do, may the luck of the Irish be there with you.

A man in love is incomplete until he has married, then he is finished.

An Irishman is never drunk as long as he can hold onto one blade of grass to keep from falling off the earth.

A hair on the head is worth two on the brush.—Oliver Herford

God is good to the Irish, but no one else is; not even the Irish.

My mother's menu consisted of two choices: Take it or leave it.

Everyone is wise until he speaks.

Irish Drinking Toasts

The Irish forgive their great men when they are safely buried.

Every St Patrick's Day, every Irishman goes out to find another Irishman to make a speech to.

Cheaters never prosper, unless they get away with it.

May the curse of Mary Malone and her nine blind illegitimate children chase you so far over the hills of Damnation that the Lord himself can't find you with a telescope.—Unknown

There are three types of people in this world: those who make things happen, those who watch things happen, and those who wonder what happened.—Unknown

I can resist everything except temptation.—Oscar Wilde

The quickest way to double your money is to fold it in half and put it back in your pocket.

Happy At the Hairy

Well, the Hairy Lemon I've been to to twice
I wish I could say I thought it was nice
But nice is too boring a word I could use
For this heavenly, mouthwatering, wonderful food.

I shall tell you about the food and drink first
Because the house wine they served really quenched my thirst
The Beef Nachos were nothing less than Divine
And the complimentary bread and butter pudding was more than just fine

The most memorable experiences I had though by far
Was the family who run this fantastic restaurant and bar
The two brothers there are Darren and Simon
Melissa the sister, a rare gem you will find in

So whether your coming to Dublin from a far away place
Or like me, live here and want some beautiful space
Be sure to the Hairy Lemon Restaurant you come
I guarantee you will remember the food and the fun.

Grainne Savage

THE FAMILY

Michael & Kathleen Bacon

Melissa Cooper, Simon Cooper, Angela Cooper and Annette Cooke

Angela Cooper and Annette Cooke

Melissa Cooper

Darren Cooper

Angela Cooper and Simon Cooper

Starters / Pickers / Sharers

Homemade Vegetable Soup (v) ●●●
using fresh seasonal vegetables served with homemade brown bread

Seafood Chowder ●●●●
a creamy potato & dill soup with fresh fish, mussels & brown bread

Dublin Bay Seafood ●●●
Donegal squid medley of prawns & mussels in a white wine & cream sauce served with brown bread

Donegal Squid (Calamari rings) ●●●
Served with a wedge of lemon & a basil aioli dip

Voodoo Chicken Wings ●●●
with a Cashel blue cheese dip

Nacho Platter (c)
topped with chilli beef, melted Irish cheddar, salsa, guacamole, sour cream & jalapeno peppers

Garlic Bread
topped with Dubliner cheddar cheese

Bruschetta (v)
topped with marinated tomatoes, onions extra virgin olive oil & basil

House Salad (v)
Green leaf salad

Homemade Onion Rings (v) ●

Chunky Chips (v) ●
with chilli & mayo dip

Curry chips (v) ●●●

Potato Wedges (v) ●●
with chilli & mayo dip

Potato Wedges ●●●
with bacon & Dubliner Cheddar Cheese

Dips ●
soy, garlic, gravy, curry, hot sauce, sweet chilli, sour cream, caramelised onions, jalapenos, cashel blue cheese, guacamole

All Day Traditional Irish Breakfast

Full Irish Breakfast ●●●
with sausages, bacon, egg, black & white pudding, tomato, mushrooms, beans & toast.

Served with fries
FREE TEA or REGULAR COFFEE

*Vegetarian option available

Burgers / Steaks / Sandwiches

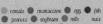

Butchers Choice 10oz Steak (c) ●●●
served with crispy fried onions with home cut chips & pepper sauce or garlic butter
Surf & Turf / add prawns €3.00

Sirloin Steak Sandwich with fries ●●●
on a toasted ciabatta with lettuce, tomato, caramelised onions with garlic & tomato relish

8oz Irish Beef Burger ●●●
topped with cheese , bacon , lettuce, onion , mayo & relish on a floury bap served with fries

Chicken Burger ●●
grilled breast of chicken with lettuce tomato, onion, on a floury bap served with fries

Veggie Burger ●●
veg pattie topped with lettuce, onion, mayo & relish served with fries

Add Cheese ●   €1.00

● cereals ● crustaceans ● egg ● fish
● peanuts ● soybeans ● milk ● nuts
● celery ● mustard ● sesame seeds
● sulphites ● lupin ● mollusc

Chef's Specialities

Chicken fillet roulade or goats cheese & bacon (c) ●●
Served on a bed of creamy mash with honey roast seasonal veg

Braised Lamb Shank (c) ●●
slow cooked with fresh vegetables, mash & red wine jus

Beef & Guinness Pie ●●●
tender beef reduced in red wine & Guinness with vegetables & mushrooms topped with a pastry lid served with chips & brown bread on the side

Traditional Irish Stew (c) ●●
slow cooked stew of lamb, potatoes, carrots, celery, onions & fresh herbs served with baked potato & brown bread

Famous Dublin Coddle ●●●
our recipe of bacon, sausage, root veg, potatoes & herbs in a savoury broth served with mash & brown bread

Traditional Cottage Pie (c) ●●●●
ground beef, onions, carrots in a rich stock topped with mashed potato & cheddar cheese served with brown bread & chips
Add Gravy €1.00

Traditional Bacon & Cabbage ●●
served with creamy mashed potato & parsley sauce

Bangers & Mash ●●●
Award winning, pan fried chef pork sausages served on a bed of mash with a rich red wine gravy, caramelised onions & topped with a homemade onion ring

Roast Vegetable Pie (v) ●●●
selection of roasted seasonal vegetables cooked in a creamy sauce topped with mash potato served with crisp salad & homemade brown bread
Add Chicken €2.00
Add Bacon €1.00

Thai Red Vegetarian Curry (c) (v) ●●
Using the freshest ingredients to deliver an aromatic curry served with jasmine infused rice
Add Half Rice/ Half Chips €1.50

Thai Red Chicken Curry (c) ●●
Succulent chunks of chicken & fresh vegetables in our coconut cream curry served with jasmine infused rice
Add Half Rice/ Half Chips €1.50
Add Dublin Bay Prawns €3.00

Fish / Salads

Salmon Supreme (c) ●●●●
fresh Atlantic Salmon served on a bed of vegetable rice with a lemon dressing

Fish & Chips ●●
Beer battered fresh cod served with mushy peas & tartare sauce
(Dry Cereals Based)

Cajun Caesar Salad ●●
Salad of mixed leaves with crispy bacon, cajun chicken, parmesan cheese & caesar dressing served with brown bread

Wild Smoked Salmon & Dublin Bay Prawn Salad ●●
served with mixed leaves, a honey & black pepper dressing & brown bread

Goats Cheese Salad ●●●●
bed of mixed leaves chopped nuts, goats cheese & caramelised onions with a honey mustard dressing & brown bread

Pasta

Fresh Seafood Pasta ●●●●
Fresh medley of seafood cooked in a creamy white wine sauce on a bed of pasta

Chicken Carbonara ●●●
chicken, bacon & mushroom on a bed of pasta in a rich creamy sauce served with garlic bread

Baked Lasagne ●●●●
served with salad, garlic bread & chips

Pasta Primavera (v) ●●●
penne pasta in a creamy sauce with mushrooms, onions, tomatoes & seasonal vegetables with garlic bread

C = suitable if you are coeliac. V = vegetarian.

If you have any specific dietary requirements or allergies, please tell your server prior to ordering & we will make any changes where possible.

At the Dairy Lemon we don't do fast food, we do great food as quick as we can, please allow 10 - 15 mins. cooking time.

97

Beverages

All hot drinks are served with homemade biscuits

Espresso
A short, black aromatic coffee traditionally enjoyed with a little sugar

Americano
A long espresso based coffee served black

White Coffee
An espresso based coffee, topped with hot steamed milk

Latte
A long, mild, milky drink with a gentle hint of espresso coffee

Mocha
A milky combination of chocolate and espresso coffee

Cappuccino
A combination of espresso steamed and foamed milk, lightly dusted with chocolate flakes

Hot Chocolate
A scrumptious beverage made from steamed milk and coco

Decaffeinated Coffee
An instant coffee with the caffeine removed

Tea

Ask about our selection of Teas available

Pint of Milk / Glass of Milk

THE HAIRY LEMON

Lunch Menu
Deal Mon-Fri 12-4pm

It's in everything we do. It's in the welcome you get whenever you pay us a visit. It's in the food & drink we create & serve you. From our award-winning Irish Stew to our award-winning sausages. From our Guinness to our smooth glasses of Jameson. So enjoy your time with us and enjoy The Hairy Lemon craic!

CERTIFICATE OF EXCELLENCE 2016
CERTIFICATE OF EXCELLENCE 2015
CERTIFICATE OF EXCELLENCE 2014
CERTIFICATE OF EXCELLENCE 2013
CERTIFICATE OF EXCELLENCE 2012
CERTIFICATE OF EXCELLENCE 2011

House Stews All

Served With Freshly Baked Brown Bread

traditional irish stew; diced lamb, carrots, onions potato &
herbs in a mouth watering stew ●

famous Dublin Coddle; a savoury broth of pork sausages, bacon,
potatoes & vegetables ●●

Beef & Guinness Pie; chunks of tender beef, mushrooms &
vegetables cooked in guinness & red wine & topped
with a buttery pastry lid ●●●●

creamy seafood chowder, a medley of local seafood cooked
with diced potatoes, carrots, onions & cream ●●●

traditional cottage pie; ground beef, onions, carrots &
garden peas cooked in a rich gravy topped with mash &
cheddar cheese ●●

root vegetable pie (v) slow cooked veg cooked in a savoury
creamy sauce topped with mashed potato & parmesan cheese ●●

Hairy Lemon was one of the most
famous of all Dublin characters &
more than likely got his name from
his odd appearance. His face was
lemon-shaped with the complexion of
his skin akin to that particular fruit and stubble
of hair resembling that which grows on a
gooseberry. Hairy was seen to be roaming the
streets, catching stray dogs for the police forces.
He died in the Fifties.

pictures are for illustration purposes only

Sandwiches

b.l.t.; bacon , lettuce, tomato sandwich ●

club sandwich; chicken, bacon, lettuce, tomato
& mayo sandwich ●●

chicken twister; wrap with breaded chicken,
salad & sweet chili sauce ●●

homemade beef burger topped with lettuce,
tomato, mayo & onion ●●●
with bacon & cheese

chicken fillet burger topped with lettuce, tomato,
mayo & onion ●●●
with bacon & cheese

veggie burger topped with lettuce, tomato,
mayo & onion ●●●
with cheese

****** add House Salad ******
******* add Chips ******

● cereals ● crustaceans ● egg ● fish
● peanuts ● soybeans ● milk   nuts
● celery ● mustard ● sesame seeds
● sulphites ● lupin ● mollusc

99

Beverages

All hot drinks are served with homemade biscuits

Espresso
A short, black, aromatic coffee traditionally
enjoyed with a little sugar

Americano
A long espresso based coffee served black

White Coffee
An espresso based coffee, topped with hot steamed milk

Latte
A long, mild, milky drink with a gentle hint of espresso coffee

Mocha
A milky combination of chocolate and espresso coffee

Cappuccino
A combination of espresso steamed and foamed milk,
lightly dusted with chocolate flakes

Hot Chocolate
A scrumptious beverage made from steamed milk and coco

Decaffeinated Coffee
An instant coffee with the caffeine removed

Tea

Ask about our selection of Teas available

Pint of Milk / Glass of Milk

THE HAIRY LEMON
dessert menu

WE'RE
PROUD OF OUR
IRISH HERITAGE
AT THE HAIRY LEMON
THAT'S WHY THERE'S
A TASTE OF IRELAND
IN EVERYTHING WE
DO. IT'S IN THE WELCOME YOU
GET WHENEVER YOU PAY US
A VISIT. IT'S IN THE FOOD
AND DRINK WE SERVE TOO,
FROM OUR SAUSAGES TO OUR
IRISH STEWS AND OUR DUBLIN
CODDLES, FROM OUR
COLD PINTS OF GUINNESS
TO OUR SMOOTH GLASSES
OF JAMESON, WE'RE MORE
THAN A LITTLE IRISH AT
HEART, SO SPEND SOME
TIME WITH US ENJOY THE
CRAIC AND YOU'RE
SURE TO FEEL
THE SAME.

Great news!
The Hairy Lemon has earned a TripAdvisor
2013 Certificate of Excellence
This prestigious award, which places us in the top-performing
10% of all businesses worldwide on TripAdvisor,
is given to businesses that consistently earn high ratings from
TripAdvisor travellers.

 tripadvisor®   Menupages.ie f

WWW.THEHAIRYLEMON.IE
DESIGN & PRINT BY JUST-PRINT.IE T. 01 494 0222 E. INFO@JUST-PRINT.IE

It's in everything we do. It's in the welcome you get whenever you pay us a visit.
It's in the food & drink we create & serve you, from our award-winning Irish Stew
to our award-winning sausages. From our Guinness to our smooth glasses of Jameson,
So enjoy your time with us and enjoy The Hairy Lemon craic!

All desserts

All served with fresh cream or ice cream

Guinness Chocolate Mousse
Guinness infused chocolate mousse with a
biscuit crumble base & whipped cream topping

Traditional Bread & Butter Pudding
One of our all time favourite classic puddings
served warm with fresh custard & cream or ice cream

Chocolate Fudge Cake
Indulgent chocolate cake
served warm with vanilla ice cream

Sticky Toffee Pudding
A delicious moist toffee sponge pudding smothered
in warm dulce de leche

A home-made caramelised apple tart
served with fresh cream or ice cream
and creme anglaise

Irish Baileys cream cheesecake
served with fresh cream or ice cream

Selection of Ice Cream (Gluten Free)
Vanilla, chocolate or strawberry ice cream
topped with chopped nuts
& caramel sauce

Hairy Lemon was one of the most
famous of all Dublin characters &
more than likely got his name from
his odd appearance. His face was
lemon-shaped with the complexion of
his skin akin to that particular fruit and stubble
of hair resembling that which grows on a
gooseberry. Hairy was seen to be roaming the
streets, catching stray dogs for the police forces.
He died in the fifties.

*pictures are for illustration purposes only

KEEP CALM AND LISTEN TO IRISH MUSIC

As you slide down the banister of life, May the splinters never point in the wrong direction!
~An Irish Saying

Irish Music

TRAD SESSIONS
AT THE HAIRY LEMON

THE HAIRY LEMON

EVERY SUNDAY AT 7PM

94764183R00071

Made in the USA
Middletown, DE
21 October 2018